THE JAM

Acknowledgements

With very grateful thanks to Philip Dodd, Morse Modaberi,
Helen Johnson and to Michael Heatley,
Northdown Publishing and the staff of the National
Sound Archive for their help in the research of this book.

Richard Lowe was a music and lifestyle journalist before leaving
Smash Hits magazine, where he was Editor between 1989 and
1991. Since leaving *Smash Hits* he has been writing for a
variety of magazines including *Q*, *Mojo* and *Select*.

First published in 1997 by
Virgin Publishing Ltd
332 Ladbroke Grove
London W10 5AH.

Modern Icons series conceived and developed
for and with Virgin Publishing Ltd by Flame Tree Publishing,
a part of The Foundry Creative Media Company Limited,
The Long House, Antrobus Road, Chiswick, London W4 5HY.

ISBN 1 85227 663 0

A catalogue record for this book is available from the British Library.

Virgin MoDERN iCoNS

THE JAM

Introduction by Richard Lowe

CONTENTS

CONTENTS

INTRODUCTION

T he best pop music comes in hit singles, seven inch slabs of vinyl that play at 45 rpm and race to the top of the charts. The best pop music speaks volumes – even if it's indirectly – of the time and place in which it was made. The best pop groups are well-dressed, glamorous, stars; they have energy, passion and heart. And the best pop groups quit while they're ahead, go out with a bang, never fade away.

By all these criteria The Jam were the best. In five years, they released sixteen singles, all of them hits, most of them perfect. They played them on *Top Of The Pops,* decked out in their immaculate Mod finery, with a fury and fire that put the rest to shame. They said everything that needed to be said about growing up in Britain in the late Seventies – every teenage neurosis addressed, every statue kicked over. And they bowed out at the top, with an unstoppable number one single, the biggest band in the country, when their leader was still only 23. They were perfect. The holy trinity. Paul, Bruce and Rick . . . . The Jam.

Their origins were inauspicious. They were from Woking, a sleepy, dreary Surrey commuter town famed only for having the biggest cemetery in Europe. And they were your typical schoolboy band of the time – a shifting line-up knocking out ham-fisted covers of 'Roll Over Beethoven' and 'Johnny B. Goode' in the school music room, scratching around for

opportunities to play to bored drinkers in the local working men's clubs.

The difference between The Jam, and the hundred, thousands of similar schoolboy dabblers, was Paul Weller. Focused, fanatical, devoted – with a blind faith in his ultimate success that at that stage was entirely unfounded – he was consumed by twin passions, music and clothes, to the exclusion of everything else. He's not changed much since.

He was the school's sharpest dresser, a Suedehead with the full wardrobe of Ben Shermans, Sta-prest, Harringtons, brogues. He was also the most curious, most obsessive, music fan, a Beatles fanatic and a young devotee of the Northern Soul nights held at Woking Football Club and nearby Bisley Pavilion. Some time in 1974 he stumbled across a song – on his little sister's soundtrack album of the David Essex film *Stardust* – that blew him away. One listen to The Who's 'My Generation', that adrenalin-rush anthem of teenage arrogance and frustration and Weller was hooked. He was a Mod.

With the single-minded dedication characteristic of him to this day he explored every aspect of this long-gone Sixties youth cult. It didn't so much transform his tastes as crystallise them, bringing everything into sharp focus. Suddenly there was a smart, aggressive alternative to the shallow glam rock that was the staple of the era. He devoured the mod musical heritage – The Who, The Small Faces, The Creation, The Kinks, The Action, Tamla Motown, Sixties soul – and set about moulding the group in the image of what he now saw as his direct forbears. He bought a Lambretta, a parka, the full uniform. In 1975 he must have stuck out like a sore thumb. Within five years a significant proportion of the teenage population of Britain would be trailing in his wake, sporting Fred Perries, bowling shoes and three-button tunic suits.

By this time The Jam had a settled line-up – Weller on guitar and vocals, Bruce Foxton on bass, Rick Buckler on drums – and were

keen to make their way onto the London club circuit. It was here they came across Dr Feelgood, one of the mainstays of the then flourishing London pub-rock circuit, a slew of bands, who, in reaction to the pomp, pretensions and excess of 'progressive' rock, had re-activated good-time, no frills R'n'B. The Feelgoods were rough, raucous and frenetic, and their guitarist Wilko Johnson played with a fierce energy and skill that deeply impressed Weller.

These two profound influences transformed The Jam. They acquired their trademark mod crops, black suits and white shirts, Weller and Foxton bought matching red Rickenbacker guitars in homage to Pete Townshend and the fire of their playing set them apart from the tame, tepid acts who were their peers on the Surrey club circuit. They were ready for London. And they were ready for punk rock.

The blossoming of The Jam into a tight, cohesive, visually striking group with its own (albeit heavily derivative) sound coincided neatly with the punk rock explosion that detonated in London in 1976. For The Jam it was the final piece of the jigsaw: a scene of young bands playing to young audiences that they could be a part of, and an ideological movement that they could instantly adopt and adapt. The Clash's set was essentially a bleak commentary on contemporary urban life and a seething tirade of invective against those responsible for it – the teachers, the politicians, the police. Suddenly mewling love songs, no matter how furiously bashed out, weren't good enough.

The punk rock scene itself instantly inspired Weller's first great song, the soon-to-be abbreviated 'In The City There's A Thousand Things I Want To Say To You', and the Clash influence was transparent on other new (and rather ropier) additions to The Jam's set ('Brick And Mortar', 'Time For Truth'). Another, 'Sounds From The Street', was Weller's declaration of kinship with punk but hinted at the uneasy, mutually suspicious, relationship between The Jam and the punk scene, which might simply see the three Woking boys as frauds.

While punk rock derived its credibility from being the angry voice of the young working-class 'kids from the street', its origins were rather more complicated. The Sex Pistols, were, at least in the beginning, an art school prank, moulded and masterminded by a Kings Road fashion fop, Malcolm McLaren. The Clash were fronted by a man who, as well as being longer in the tooth than was appropriate for punk's primary propagandist, was both ex-public school and ex-pub rock. The Stranglers and The Vibrators were again pub-rock stalwarts who re-invented themselves overnight when they saw which way the wind was blowing.

Yet The Jam — genuinely young, genuinely working-class — and the punk cognoscenti were uneasy bedfellows. They were fast and furious enough for some, but too conservative, too rooted in the past in both dress and sound, for others. Weller took umbrage at this partial rejection and deliberately got up the noses of those he saw as phoney. The Jam stuck resolutely to their Mod dress code and spoke unapologetically of their love for the Beatles (a punk heresy). And Weller offended punk's political correctness by making tactless remarks about his intention to vote Conservative and laying benefit gigs in celebration of the Queen's Jubilee year. He later admitted that he wanted the trendies to hate The Jam — and he succeeded.

Weller's chirpy and contrary nature, his refusal to go with the flow, would become an important part of his appeal. Even when The Jam were the biggest band in Britain, with that rare combination of commercial clout and critical acclaim, he was still the misfit, sniping from the sidelines at the fallibilities of his contemporaries. And in his first real masterpiece, 'Away From The Numbers', the highlight of The Jam's debut album 'In The City', he cast himself in this role. While the rest of the album adhered strictly to the punk rock template – loud, ragged Mod pop noise played at breakneck speed – 'Away From The Numbers' strayed from the formula. Originally conceived as

a surf-styled song (vestiges of its Beach Boys influence remain in the cooing harmonies of the middle eight), it was an anthem for the wild-hearted outsider, a precise, powerful articulation of the individualist teenager's horror of suffocating conformity. While his punk rock contemporaries may have been making all the noise with their scattergun sloganeering, Weller was proving himself to have the sniper's sharpness and cunning. He just needed the single bullet. Straight to the heart.

'Away From The Numbers' was also a harbinger of things to come. A deep streak of romanticism and a penchant for maudlin introspection would characterise Weller's work from then until now, but it sat uneasily with the punk rock purists by now at the helm of the music press. The backlash came swiftly for The Jam. Amidst the crashing powerchords of the follow-up single 'All Around The World', Weller expressed his contempt for punk rock ideology, and spelled out this hostility even more clearly in interviews.

Not surprisingly, when The Jam released their hurriedly written and recorded second album, 'This Is The Modern World', the vultures were swift to pounce. Although it had its moments – 'The Modern World', Weller's snarling put-down to any teacher, rock critic or anyone who had ever put him down, set to a riff pinched from The Who's 'Pictures Of Lily'; the two moody ballads 'Life From A Window' and 'I Need You' – it wasn't up to scratch.

And suddenly The Jam were in disarray. Critically savaged, commercially wanting (the Bruce Foxton-penned single 'News Of The World' had failed to match the chart position of its predecessors) and with Weller distracted by an obsessive, tempestuous relationship with his new girlfriend Gill Price, they set to work on their third LP. The set of songs they eventually came up with were rubbished and rejected by their producer Chris Parry. Weller admitted his ideas had dried up. But the rejection hit him hard and spurred him into action. His search for a new direction took him back to his heroes, in particular Pete Townshend and Ray Davies. Behind both writers' best songs was the same technique: the use of stories and characters to make social observations. After The Jam had swiftly whipped off a version of The Kinks's 'David Watts', a commercial stalling operation, Weller set to work.

Within weeks he'd come up with a set of sharp, witty mini soap operas, as acutely observed as those of his heroes and with added snarl and bite. There was 'Mr. Clean', a nasty, vitriolic swipe at the smug, suburban city gent; 'Billy Hunt', a mocking if friendly portrayal of a cocksure but downtrodden macho fantasist; 'To Be Someone', a sad, snide tale of the rise and fall of a rock star; and two powerful, chilling descriptions of urban violence, 'A Bomb In Wardour Street' and 'Down In The Tube Station At Midnight'.

Musically, too, The Jam had moved on in leaps and bounds.

Their stodgy 4/4 powerchord thrash had evolved into a lither, more loose-limbed sound which (although still wearing its influences proudly on its sleeve) was unmistakeably their own. The drippy acoustic ballad 'English Rose' had punk rockers reeling in horror, and another shamelessly romantic love song, 'Fly', demonstrated that in terms of ambition and sophistication, Weller as a composer had left his punk peers way behind.

'All Mod Cons' was instantly hailed as a classic. 'Tube Station' became The Jam's biggest chart hit to date and suddenly, from the brink of disaster, The Jam had catapulted themselves to the top of the pile. The Sex Pistols had fallen apart, The Clash hadn't lived up to their early promise, and by the end of 1979 The Jam were sweeping the board in the all-important NME Readers' Poll. By then they'd followed up 'All Mod Cons' with a hat-trick of peerless, priceless hit singles – 'Strange Town', 'When You're Young', 'The Eton Rifles' – and an even more ambitious album, 'Setting Sons', if ultimately not quite on a par with its predecessor. What's more, they'd unwittingly sparked a Mod revival, a movement they were reluctant to endorse whole-heartedly, given its rather dodgy nature: ugly parkas, second-rate groups, mindless violence.

By the time they released their tenth single, 'Going Underground', in May 1980, The Jam's steadily swelling army of fans was such a mighty force that they launched it straight to Number One in its first week, a feat commonplace these days but at the time extremely rare – it hadn't been done since Slade in the early Seventies.

The Jam, whether they liked it or not, were now bona fide pop stars, but it was a status that sat awkwardly with the group. They'd bought into one of the basic punk tenets: that the barriers between the star and the fans should be demolished, that all were equal in the new musical revolution. And they were at pains to play fair by their fans. They kept ticket prices low, made all their records value for money (some of The Jam's finest moments are to be found on their B-sides)

and even at the height of their fame were letting the fans into the afternoon soundchecks on tour and signing autographs until the last one had left.

Weller, in particular, was the focus for this adoration. Passionate, principled, brave, heroic, tough, intense, effortlessly glamorous, he was the sussed, cool fantasy older brother for a generation of teenage boys. The Jam were, again much to their frustration, essentially a boys' band. And it made Weller uneasy.

The spectacular success of 'Going Underground' was a turning point for The Jam, a commercial peak and a creative watershed. They'd never again release a single in that familiar Jam mould. While it would have been easy to rest on their laurels, stick with the formula and milk the rewards, such complacent commercialism disgusted Weller. Instead their restless leader chose to splinter The Jam sound into a variety of new directions. The next single was the stark, edgy 'Start!', a pop record

about communicating through pop records, another Number One. The next album, 'Sound Affects', contained alongside familiar Jam classics, strange dub-influenced dance music. And the single that followed it, 'Funeral Pyre', was The Jam's least commercial of all, a dark, dense maelstrom of ugly guitar and thundering drums.

By now The Jam, although still the most successful band in Britain, were beginning to sound dated. A new era in British pop, the most ghastly New Romantic movement of bright, colourful synth-driven dance music, was in full swing. The Jam's fans despised it of course, but Weller was taken with some of its aspects: rooted as it was in black dance music, he recognised that the London club scene that spawned the New Romantics had more in common with the Sixties Mod era than did Rickenbacker powerchords and green parkas.

A parallel development was Weller's increasingly pronounced political stance. Most artists mellow out or become bland as they grow older or more successful, Weller simply got angrier. More politically focused than ever, the group played a series of benefits for both CND and various Right To Work campaigns, and the centrepiece of the next, and final, Jam album 'The Gift', was his most urgent, direct political song to date, the messy 'Transglobal Unity Express'.

After the relatively lean year that was 1981 (only two singles and no tour) The Jam stormed back in 1982 with a double A-sided single, 'A Town Called Malice/Precious'. 'Malice' was adored by the fans – the familiar Jam sound set to a Motown backbeat, but 'Precious', with its funk rhythms, horn stabs, wah wah guitar and bassline lifted from white-funksters Pigbag, puzzled and irritated many of the group's faithful devotees.

It was this insurmountable conservatism on the part of a large proportion of their fans that frustrated Weller and, within a few months, led him to disband The Jam. A passionate believer in the power of pop music to educate, motivate and make people think, he did not have in mind the blind, dumb fan worship that The Jam attracted. By now a skilful, imaginative musician, eager to pursue new directions, the three-chord Mod pop that the audience wanted from him simply bored Weller. It was time to call it a day. But not before one last classic, the stomping celebratory swansong, 'Beat Surrender'.

Richard Lowe

21

BEAT SURRENDER

On 30 October 1982, Paul Weller unilaterally brought The Jam's career to an end. The band would complete one final tour before formally splitting.

At the end of this year, The Jam will be officially splitting up as I feel we have achieved all we can together as a group. I'd hate us to end up old and embarrassing like so many other groups do. I want us to finish with dignity.

Official press release

The difference between The Jam and all the hopeless pop ephemeralities is the difference between a (red) Harrington and an anorak. The Jam were the best.

X. Moore, NME

It's going to sound pompous anyway, but I think that we've shown that you can be successful, hugely successful, which we are, do that and still remain decent, still remain caring and honest.

Paul Weller, Melody Maker, November 1982

Rick and Bruce were a bit
shocked really, but I think
after a while they'll see that
what I'm saying is right.
Paul Weller, *Melody Maker,*
November 1982

*Weller's decision had come as
something of a bolt from the
blue to his two colleagues,
bass player Bruce Foxton and
drummer Rick Buckler. In 1992,
the two would sue for some
£200,000 of royalties and
merchandising income.*

I couldn't understand Paul's reasons, at the time. After working with someone for nine years, it was still difficult to actually realise what he deep down inside felt.

Bruce Foxton, *Jamming,* 1983

Thanks for all your support over the past years.
I'm going to miss you.

Rick Buckler, in the final tour programme

Behind Weller's announcement was
his oft-quoted concern not to end up
recycling past glories like the
'dinosaur' acts that he despised.

The worst thing about it is that these
people have been going on and on about
being spokesmen for a generation. How
can you be that if you live in the South of
France ten months out of the year?

Paul Weller, *Melody Maker,* 1977

It was quite a hard decision. Really, it was
the thought of us continuing that I found
more frightening. I wouldn't like to be
going out on stage singing 'When You're
Young' when I'm fuckin' 30 or something.

Paul Weller, *NME,* 1982

You can't play rock'n'roll
when you've got a beer gut.

Paul Weller, *NME,* 1977

And when The Jam broke up, Paul Weller would go on, via the jazz-tinged cul-de-sac of the Style Council, to re-emerge as the Godfather of Britpop.

There are people out there the same age as me – thirty five years old with two kids who met their wife at a Jam gig in '79. We've all grown up together and we've been through a lot. As long as it doesn't get too nostalgic or sentimental, I'm happy.
Paul Weller

I only listen to The Jam if it comes up on the radio or something and it sounds really dated now.
Paul Weller, Q magazine, 1988

THE MODFATHERS

Weller, Foxton and Buckler all had one thing in common: the Surrey town of Woking and its Sheerwater County Secondary School. The band grew out of a group of Paul's school friends who jammed together – hence the name – during school lunchbreaks.

We weren't hip at all. We came from Woking, for a start. I thought punk was the first working-class musical movement in my time, that's how I perceived it. And I think that's why The Jam clicked. We made our own scene.

Paul Weller, *Mojo,* 1975

It was quite cliquey and elitist in a London way. They were really hip, and we weren't, we were just three green kids from Woking, from a little hick town.

Paul Weller, after an early Jam gig at The Roxy.

The early Seventies were the tag end of the hippy era. Loon pants and Afghan coats were not for working-class lads from Woking. Paul Weller heard The Who's 'My Generation' on his sister's copy of the 'Stardust' soundtrack album, and he discovered a way of life.

It's like a code, in a way. It gives something to my life . . . . I'm still a Mod. I'll always be a Mod. You can bury me a Mod.

Paul Weller, 1991

This is more than Grade B punning or a clever-clever link-up with the nostalgibuzz packaging (like the target design on the label, the swinging London trinkery, the Lambretta diagram or the Immediate-style lettering); it's a direct reference to the broadening of musical idiom and Weller's reaffirmation of a specific Mod consciousness.

Charles Shaar Murray on 'All Mod Cons', *NME,* 1978

I think people thought I was a bit eccentric. It must have been weird to see me driving around on a scooter with a Parka on in 1975.

Paul Weller, *Mojo,* 1995

*Despite the Mod influence,
Paul Weller always angrily
rejected claims that The Jam
were simply a Mod revival.*

It just bores the arse off me. Just
another movement like the skinheads
and punks. There are already a
load of Mod bands like the Ricky Tics
from Nottingham, The Purple Hearts
from Barking, The Scooters from
Coventry and I wish them all luck,
but I'm not pledging my allegiance
to any movement . . . . We're not
reviving anything and we're as
influenced by contemporary bands
as much as anything else. I still love
all the Pistols singles.
Paul Weller, *Zigzag,* 1977

A lot of retards assume they're
some kind of revival band –
which is just so far removed
from the truth it's incredible.
Tony Parsons, *NME,* 1977

SPREADING THE JAM

*Of the three Jam members, there was little
doubt who was the leader of the band.
Although Bruce Foxton did some songwriting,
Weller was the mainspring and the inspiration,
although his early political position caused
him some later embarrassment.*

Favourite single – 'My Girl', Otis Redding.
Favourite album – 'My Generation', The Who.
Influence – Tamla Motown.
The Jam File, *Melody Maker,* 1977

She's the best diplomat we've got. She works harder
than what you or I do or the rest of the country.
Paul Weller on the Queen, *NME,* 1977 –
the interview in which he declared he'd vote Conservative

Disastrous! I still get asked about that;
 it's the worst part of my history.
An older, rueful **Paul Weller**

MoDERN iCoNS — THE JAM

*Bruce Foxton originally joined
The Jam as rhythm guitarist,
moving to bass when Paul's
schoolfriend Steve Brookes
dropped out of the band.*

Favourite single – 'My Cherie
Amour', Stevie Wonder.
Favourite album – 'My
Generation', The Who.
Influence – Tamla Motown.
The Jam File, *Melody Maker,* 1977

Foxton runs up the
monitors or moves like a
blind crab whose emo-
tional turmoil you can, as
always, perceive by his
constantly changing
facial expressions.
Tony Parsons, *NME,* 1977

One thing I do know is that
when the Jam fall through I
ain't gonna join another
band. This is the only band
I'll ever play with.
Bruce Foxton, *Sounds,* 1978

39

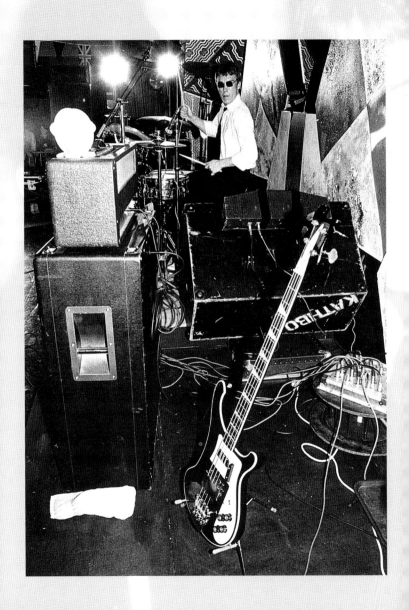

Rick Buckler's original musical influence had been heavy rock – he was already an accomplished drummer by the time he was drafted into the band.

Favourite single – 'Stayed Awake All Night',
Bachman Turner Overdrive.
Favourite album – 'Tommy', The Who.
Influence – Paul Hammond.
The Jam File, *Melody Maker,* 1977

Rick Buckler hangs tough behind his kit, cool as a spring breeze, snapping out a precise beat with contemptuous ease. The kind of drummer that makes me want to up and trade my guitar for a drum kit immediately! If Jimmy Dean had been a drummer he would've played like Rick Buckler.
John Hamblett, *NME,* 1977

With their Rickenbackers, Vox AC30s, and black-suited high energy, The Jam broke out of Woking's club circuit under the guidance of their manager, Weller's father John.

Most R&R Maximum R&B.

Flier for The Jam appearing at The Greyhound, London, March 1976

With bands far exceeding the number of London clubs, sometimes you *really* have to take it to the streets. Last Saturday, The Jam did just that. Setting up on the pavement outside Soho Market about 12.30, they ripped it up for almost an hour. A small, appreciative crowd developed, complete with beggar.

John Ingham, *NME,*
October 1976 on an al fresco showcase

You will love this band (and that's an order).
NME headline, May 1977

INFLUENCES

I ain't rock'n'roll. It's boring. Rock'n'roll's been dead for years. It died when Elvis went into the army.
Paul Weller, *Zigzag,* 1979

Paul first picked up on The Beatles, played incessantly by his mother. He held a jumble sale in his bedroom and bought a copy of 'Sgt Pepper'.

He was Beatles mad. He's got every *Beatles Monthly.* Paul's got the original collection.
Nicky Weller, Paul's sister

It really caught my imagination – it's a very colourful record. I just thought the sound on it was fantastic and I couldn't understand how people had created that sound, and that intrigued me.

Paul Weller, Q magazine, 1995, on "the record that changed my life": 'Strawberry Fields Forever'

As part of Weller's immersion in Mod Culture, required listening included The Small Faces's output, but above all, The Who. The B-side of 'Down In The Tube Station At Midnight' was The Who's 'So Sad About Us', the Jam's tribute to the recently departed Keith Moon.

This was the record that changed my life. It was a massive influence. I've plagiarised the whole album, I think – I just changed the titles!

Paul Weller on The Who's 'My Generation'

Weller's chording is inspired, he skitters in early Townshend feedback licks with ease.

Phil McNeill, *NME,* on 'In The City'

When Weller and Townshend finally met, in 1980, the occasion proved something of an anti-climax.

The great meeting that never was. The comparison between us was finally broken for good as we discovered we really had nothing in common. I still respect the man though for his honesty above all else.

Paul Weller, *Melody Maker,* 1983

Along with the Mod bands came plenty of R&B and Motown.

R&B, Wilson Picket, Otis Redding. I still find that the most satisfying music. I still think a load of the Sixties bands were a lot more creative than most around now.
Paul Weller, *Zigzag,* 1977

Years ago, when we were still in the clubs, half our set was always like Motown covers and Stax covers. So we've always really had the R&B thing.
Paul Weller, *NME,* 1982

Ray Davies of The Kinks was another strong influence. The Jam paid homage to him by releasing a cover version of his 'David Watts' in 1978.

I found myself thinking of Ray Davies. There's the same wearing your suburban neuroses on your sleeve, the same lack of over-whelming confidence, the same disbelief that somebody is paying you to do this . . . . Long may Paul Weller have such modest aims.

Pete Silverton, *Sounds,* on 'All Mod Cons'

Forget the Sixties. Forget comparisons. Forget Jam, The Who, Beatles, The Kinks. Forget the naive neurosis of the plagiarists. The Jam are here. And now.

Barry Cain, *Record Mirror* on 'This Is The Modern World'

SERIOUS STUFF

*A frequent criticism levelled at
The Jam, and Weller in particular,
was that they took themselves just
a little too seriously.*

We're not a fun band. I don't like
fun groups, groups that are just a
good laugh like the Boomtown
Rats. Without going over the top,
it's important for a group to take
themselves seriously.
Paul Weller, *Zigzag,* 1979

A lot of our songs have got
humour in them that probably
doesn't come out because people
don't go into our songs. They just
take them at face value.
Paul Weller

Another Weller attribute was his habit of telling journalists exactly what was in his mind . . .

I'd be too embarrassed to write something like 'We're all going down the pub', even though that is probably real to thousands of kids, and very truthful. I just feel that I should reach for something higher.
NME, 1978

People say that I'm arrogant and big-headed about everything that we do, but it's not really true. I only like doing stuff that we think is really good.
Zigzag, 1979

Pop stars are generally one of the most self-centred, unhealthy, big-headed bunch of wankers around, so why should I wish to be associated with people like that?
Jamming, 1981

As an adjunct to The Jam's musical activities, Paul Weller set up a publishing house, Riot Stories, in 1979. Now relinquishing his youthful Conservatism, he was becoming as serious about his political beliefs as he was about his music.

I don't have an extravagant lifestyle. I haven't got any mansion, just a two-roomed flat, I haven't got a car and I do my own shopping.

Paul Weller, *Record Mirror,* 1982

Nothing will be achieved all
the time we remain separated,
but together we can win.
Paul Weller, on BBC1's
Nationwide, on CND

I find it really hard to listen
to them early LPs. I think my
big mistake really, which
was a little bit of naivety,
was trying to do political
lyrics at that stage. I was
really influenced by the
Clash, their early things.
And I just had a go at
doing them.
Paul Weller, *NME,* 1982

*Behind the polemic, the skilled songwriter garnered
critical acclaim, and thought hard about his chosen craft.*

Weller has the almost unique ability to write love songs
that convince the listener that the singer is *really in love*.
Chas de Whalley, *Sounds,* on 'This Is The Modern World'

I've always said we're a pop band; I
like pop music. I mean I've always said I like
tunes and melody, so there's no compromise at all.
Paul Weller, *Zigzag,* 1977

'That's Entertainment' must rate as one of Paul
Weller's finest pieces to date. He's observing with more
vivid descriptions than at any time previously . . . .
As always the view point is a humane, personalistic
one. I've got 'Sound Affects' and I'm chuffed with it
and all I want now is another Jam album.
Paul Du Noyer, *NME*

When I was in The Jam, I wrote about other people's
feelings. Now I write about myself, my feelings.
Paul Weller, 1994

THE LOOK

The classic Jam look was an immediate descendent of Dr Feelgood's image as portrayed on the Canvey Island band's debut album 'Down By The Jetty'.

The front cover, depicting four mean-looking, short-haired dudes in natty suits, was matched by the ferocious, jittery R&B in the album's grooves.

Journalist **Nigel Cross**, 1996

We found that this was the sort of music we liked playing, and the way we liked to dress, and the whole thing grew from there. We didn't say, 'This is a good image, we'll do it'. It just developed naturally.

Bruce Foxton

The Jam adopted the 'Down By The Jetty' uniform, press-ganged by Paul into going down to their local Burtons to be fitted for the regulation black suits. Cropped hair was de rigueur (although Foxton never quite went the whole hog) and Buckler added some mean shades.

To me the Mod dress is a private thing anyway. Rick and Bruce aren't into it really.
Paul Weller, *Zigzag,* 1979

Yup, they wear snazzy clothes, have their hair razor cut and even ride about on scooters.
Melody Maker, 1977

63

*The Jam army of fans reached its peak in 1979
along with the emergence of Mod bands like Purple
Hearts, Secret Affair and the Merton Parkas (featuring
Weller's future Style Council partner Mick Talbot).*

The mod image is not that important to The Jam. It's more
important to me personally, because that's what I am.
Paul Weller, *NME,* 1978

The Jam's fans are in the process of re-organising their
transport and, in the true spirit of Mods, are planning to

get scooters complete with
wing mirrors . . . . They're
all as much into the
complete Sixties fashion
as they are into the band.
Record Mirror, 1978

It was frightening, the
hysteria when The Jam
were at their peak.
Paul Weller, *Mojo,* 1995

Perhaps because the sound and the image were just too British, The Jam never broke America, although they tried, but gained cult status as an Anglophile speciality.

The Jam is about to submerge America in the New Wave.
Polydor ad 1978

I don't think you've had the same thing in America, but we've always had these little fads based around music and clothes . . . . It may seem strange to Americans, but in England there's a need for that kind of expression – because there's nothing else.
Paul Weller, *Musician* magazine

THE PUNK THING

The Jam came forth at the same time as the whole Punk movement. There was a connection they acknowledged but never fully embraced.

They weren't seen as part of what was happening, but nothing was really happening at that stage. They were part of what wasn't happening. They were different enough – they were young and they played three-minute songs.

Sex Pistols bassist, **Glen Matlock**

I could tell you things that Rotten and Strummer have said to me that would show their major aims are just to be stars and make lots of money.

Paul Weller, *NME,* 1977

The anarchic attitude of punk found a resonance in The Jam's youthful aggression.

They sparked the whole thing off. Not that we're very much associated with them, but they still did a lot for the music. They brought about a lot of change. They frightened some of the older musicians which is a good thing.
Paul Weller on the Sex Pistols, *NME*, 1977

I feel that the mod scene was very close to the punk thing: wholly youth – like going out with green hair. It changed you, made you someone. I thought that was the most important aspect of punk.
Paul Weller, *NME*, 1978

*But when The Jam had drawn
what they needed from the punk
revolution, they simply moved on.*

I think we all used to believe in rock
when we started off. Like punk rock.
Over the last few years I've realised what
a lot of shit it all is. All this rebel stance.
Paul Weller, *Melody Maker,* 1982

The Jam bear no relation to the
mass conception of punk . . . . The
Weller compositions are anything
but an embarrassment. He has a
deft touch that places his material
on a much higher plateau.
Brian Harrigan, *Melody Maker*

Paul Weller would have made
it with or without the New Wave.
Bob Edwards, *NME, 1977*

Despite his reservations about punk, Paul Weller mourned its passing, especially when the early Eighties saw the pendulum swing back.

It's like punk never happened. I think there should be music with some kind of sensibilities, some kind of consciousness, instead of this showbiz crap like Adam Ant wants to bring back.

Paul Weller, *Record Mirror,* 1982

My attitude towards the whole thing about being successful – however clichéd this sounds – really did change when I saw the Sex Pistols and the Clash in '76. I think those bands realised that there was more you could do with success than just use it as a way out. It could be used in a more positive direction.

Paul Weller, *Hot Press,* 1981

MUSICAL MOMENTS

The Jam's first single and album were both entitled 'In The City' and announced the band's arrival on the 1977 music scene with vigour and vim.

His songs change key, change back, go from silence to hammer riffs, capture that entire teen frustration vibe with the melodic grace and dynamic aplomb of early Kinks and Who.

Phil McNeill, *NME*

'In The City' kicks off side two. This'll always be The Jam's classic, the one they'll have to do onstage forever. It's got the lot this track – melody, drive, a bloody great riff, all delivered with maximum exuberance.

Zigzag

I thought it was a great debut album. It was rough, but that's how we were at the time. It was how it should be.

Paul Weller, October 1977

A landmark release was the October 1978 single 'Down In The Tube Station At Midnight', a tight three-minute scenario of urban violence: a commuter is attacked by drunken fascists.

If Eisenstein made 45s they'd sound like this . . .
John Cooper Clarke, *Record Mirror*

I think it's disgusting the way these punks sing about violence all the time. Why can't they sing about beautiful things like trees and flowers?
DJ **Tony Blackburn**

Pop artists brought into art everyday images that people could relate to. That's basically what I'm doing – taking an everyday situation, like a tube station, and turning it into art.
Paul Weller, 1978

*'Eton Rifles', the November 1979
single taken from 'Setting Sons'
crashed into the UK charts at Number
3, and marked the arrival of The Jam
as a successful chart band (their next
two singles hit Number 1).*

I saw this TV programme and thought it
was a good title. But the actual song is
just a piss-take of the class system. I
mean, I'm a very class-conscious person.
I realise it's a joke and it shouldn't really
exist in the Eighties but it still does.
Paul Weller, *The Story So Far* magazine

Nobody's allowed to be this good.
Noel Gallagher on hearing
'Eton Rifles' for the first time

Do you remember there was a Right to
Work March a few years back that went
through Eton? There was a little skirmish
there, all about that song.
Paul Weller, *NME,* 1982

Towards the end of The Jam's career, there was a marked return to the Motown and R&B feel of their original influences, particularly on the album 'The Gift' and February 1982's Number 1 single 'A Town Called Malice' with its Tamla Motown bass riff, horns and Hammond organ.

We were trying to get funky. Before that I was a real purist and only listened to stuff before 1968. Michael Jackson's 'Off The Wall' was the album that really opened things up for me . . . the first contemporary soul album I'd liked.

Paul Weller

A magnificent howl at Thatcherite Britain.

NME

A mediocre song.
The Daily Mail

I thought that 'A Town
Called Malice' was a
really good pop record.
Paul Weller, *NME,* 1982

*The Jam's final appearance was at
Brighton Conference Centre
on 11th December 1982.*

At last, a rock career which ends with a bang,
instead of a whimper, squabble or overdose.
The manner of The Jam's leaving carries a
stamp of style and self-discipline, of honesty and
suss. I'm watching them go with a nice balance
of feelings: half respect and half relief. Just right.

Paul Du Noyer, *NME,* 1982

Ultimately it was the audience who let them
down, by throwing bottles and rubbish,
prompting an angry Bruce Foxton to shout:
'I want to remember this last gig for the
good moments, not the bottles'.

Paolo Hewitt, *Melody Maker,* 1982

We fuckin' meant it, and a lot of other bands
don't. And I just think that if there's any
significance, it's just that we're one of the first
groups to ever do that. I don't think there are
any other bands that have done that.

Paul Weller, *NME,* 1982

84

THE MUSIC

★★★★★   Essential listening
★★★   OK
★   Frankly, not the best!

SINGLES

In The City/Takin' My Love – April 1977 ★★★★

All Around The World/Carnaby Street – July 1977 ★★★1/2

News Of The World/Aunties & Uncles/Innocent Man – February 1978 ★★★

Down In The Tube Station At Midnight/So Sad About Us/The Night
– October 1978 ★★★★

Strange Town/The Butterfly Collector – March 1979 ★★★1/2

When You're Young/Smithers-Jones – August 1979 ★★★★

Eton Rifles/See-Saw – October 1979 ★★★★★

Going Underground/The Dreams Of Children – February 1980 ★★★★★

Start/Liza Radley – August 1980 ★★★★1/2

Funeral Pyre/Disguises – May 1981 ★★★1/2

Absolute Beginners/Tales From The Riverbank – October 1981 ★★★

A Town Called Malice/Precious – February 1982 ★★★★

The Bitterest Pill (I Ever Had To Swallow)/Pity Poor Alfie/Fever
– September 1982 ★★★★

Beat Surrender/Shopping – December 1982 ★★★★

ALBUMS

In The City — May 1977 ★★★
Sounds From The Street/In The City/Art School/Slow Down/Takin' My Love/Bricks
And Mortar/Away From The Numbers/Time For Truth/I've Changed My
Address/Batman Theme/I Got By In Time

This Is The Modern World – November 1977 ★★
Life From A Window/In The Midnight Hour/London Girl/London Traffic/The
Modern World/Here Comes The Weekend/In The Street/I Need You/Don't Tell
Them You're Sane/Tonight At Noon/Standards/The Combine/Today

All Mod Cons – November 1978 ★★★1/2
Billy Hunt/A Bomb In Wardour Street/David Watts/Fly/Down In The Tube Station
At Midnight/The Place I Love/To Be Someone/In The Crowd/It's Too Bad/English
Rose/Mr Clean/All Mod Cons

Setting Sons – November 1979 ★★★★
Thick As Thieves/The Eton Rifles/Heat Wave/Private Hell/Smithers-Jones/Burning
Skies/Girl On The Phone/Little Boy Soldiers/Saturday's Kids

Sound Affects – November 1980 ★★★★1/2
Pretty Green/That's Entertainment/Set The House Ablaze/But I'm Different
Now/Music For The Last Couple/Start/Monday/Scrape Away/Man In The Corner
Shop/Dream Time/Boy About Town

The Gift – February 1982 ★★★★
Happy Together/Town Called Malice/Precious/Carnation/Ghosts/Just Who Is The
Five O'Clock Hero/The Planner's Dream Gone Wrong/Running On The
Spot/Trans-Global Express/Circus/The Gift

Dig In The New Breed (Live 1977-1982) – December 1982 ★★
In The City/To Be Someone/It's Too Bad/Big Bird/Start/Set The House
Ablaze/Going Underground/Standards/Ghosts/Private Hell/That's
Entertainment/Dreams Of Children/In The Crowd/All Mod Cons

THE HISTORY

1973-74
The Jam starts at Sheerwater Comprehensive School in Woking, as lunch time band jamming together, hence the name. Line-up settles as Weller, Foxton, Buckler and Steve Brookes.

1975
Brookes leaves, Foxton moves to bass, Weller to guitar/lead vocals. Build up live following on the London pub circuit.

October 1976
Outdoor gig in Soho gets band attention and their first reviews in the music press.

February 1977
The Jam sign to Polydor for £6000, deal re-negotiated three months later.

April 1977
First single, 'In The City', released. A first *Top Of The Pops* appearance follows in May.

May 1977
Join the Clash 'White Riot' tour, but fall out with their management. First album released: 'In The City'.

June 1977
The Jam's first headlining UK tour begins.

August 1978
The Jam headline the Reading festival.

November 1978
'All Mod Cons' reaches Number 6 in UK charts.

November 1979
'Eton Rifles' gets to UK Number 3, and 'Setting Sons' to Number 4 in the album charts, highest positions so far.

March 1980
'Going Underground' goes straight to Number 1 and stays there for three weeks.

September 1980
'Start' also goes to Number 1. Two months later the 'Sound Affects' album reaches Number 2, and The Jam sweep the *NME* Readers' Poll.

October 1981
Weller launches *Jamming* magazine, and Respond record label.

February 1982
'A Town Called Malice/Precious' goes to Number 1. The Jam play both A and B sides on *Top Of The Pops*, the first band to do two numbers on one show since The Beatles.

October 1982
Weller announces that The Jam will split at the end of the year.

December 1982
The final single 'Beat Surrender' straight to Number 1.
Final Jam performance at Brighton Conference Centre on 11 December.

THE CAST

Steve Brookes. Born 26 May 1958, London. 'The fourth Jam'. Brookes comes from a middle-class North London family who moved to Woking in the early Seventies. Shares an obsessive love of Sixties music with Paul Weller and the two debut as a duo in 1972. Brookes stays as guitar/vocalist, but the change to the Mod look and sound proves too much. The old 'musical differences' line applies. He quits The Jam in summer 1975, eventually setting up a music shop and moving on to be a car salesman. Co-wrote first Jam A-side 'Takin' My Love'.

Rick Buckler. Born 6 December 1955 in Woking. An accomplished drummer when he joins The Jam: he is a couple of years ahead of Paul Weller at Sheerwater Secondary Modern. After the split he puts together the band Time UK with Danny Kustow (ex-Tom Robinson Band), Martin Gordon (ex-Radio Stars) and others. In 1992 joins Foxton in a £200,000 lawsuit to claim merchandising income and royalties that have accrued since the split. Retires from music in the mid-Eighties to run a furniture business.

Bruce Foxton. Born 1 September 1955 in Sheerwater, Woking. Joins The Jam in 1974 from a progressive garage band after some persuasion because of the prospect of live work. Originally a guitarist, swops to bass, allowing Weller to switch to guitar. After the Jam split he releases solo single 'Freak' (reaches UK Top 30 in 1993), solo album 'Touch Sensitive', works in a couple of combinations with Buckler, and later with the Rhythm Sisters, before joining Stiff Little Fingers.

Neil Harris. Original drummer in The Jam's first school-based manifestation. A talented local drummer, he is away when an important local gig for the fledgling Jam comes up. On his return he is out; Rick Buckler is in. Harris continues playing in dance bands on a semi-pro basis.

Chris Parry. Polydor A&R man, comes to see The Jam on recommendation of Shane McGowan. Gets The Jam onto the label, and introduces colleague Vic Smith (later Vic Coppersmith-Heaven) to the band. The latter becomes their producer.

Dave Waller. An original member of The Jam (on guitar), recruited to expand the Weller/Brookes duo. Having decided to concentrate on a career as a poet, he is replaced by Bruce Foxton in 1974. His book *Notes From A Hostile Street* is the first title released by Weller's publishing company Riot Stories in 1979. Dies in 1982 from a heroin overdose.

John Weller. Paul's father, a former amateur champion boxer, who drives The Jam as manager (literally, in the early days, in a variety of vehicles) hustles them gigs, their first record deal, and continues to manage them throughout their career – before going on to look after Paul's subsequent career.

Paul Weller. Born 25 May 1958 in Woking. After The Jam splits he hooks up with Mick Talbot to form the Style Council . . . and the rest is history.

THE BOOKS

A Beat Concerto – Paolo Hewitt (Boxtree) 1983, updated 1996
The Jam: Our Story –
      Bruce Foxton & Rick Buckler (Castle Communications) 1993
Keeping The Flame – Steve Brookes (Sterling) 1996
Paul Weller: My Ever Changing Moods –
      John Reed (Omnibus Press) 1996

PICTURE CREDITS

Pages 2-3 Neil Preston/Retna. **Page 5** Erica Echenberg/Redferns. **Page 8** Ian Dickson/Redferns. **Page 11** Simon Fowler/LFI. **Page 12** Ian Dickson/Redferns. **Page 15** Neil Preston/Retna. **Page 17** LFI. **Page 19** Neil Preston/Retna. **Page 20** Steve Morley/Redferns. **Pages 22-23** (t) Neil Preston/Retna; (b) Courtesy of Polydor Records. **Pages 24-5** Paul Cox/LFI. **Page 27** Ian Dickson/Redferns. **Page 28** A. H./Redferns. **Pages 30-31** (l) LFI; (r) Paul Cox/LFI. **Page 33** LFI. **Pages 34-5** (l) Erica Echenberg/Redferns; (r) LFI. **Page 37** Simon Fowler/LFI. **Page 38** Keith Bernstein/Redferns. **Pages 38-9** Ian Dickson/Redferns. **Page 40** Ian Dickson/Redferns. **Page 41** Paul Cox /LFI. **Page 43** LFI. **Pages 44-5** Keith Bernstein/Redferns. **Page 47** Ian Dickson/Redferns. **Page 48** LFI. **Page 49** Paul Cox/LFI. **Pages 50-1** Kevin Cummins/Retna. **Pages 52-3** LFI. **Page 54** Ebet Roberts/Redferns. **Pages 56-7** Paul Cox/LFI. **Page 58** LFI. **Pages 60-1** Ebet Roberts/Redferns. **Page 62** Ian Dickson/Redferns. **Page 64** Eugene Adebari/LFI. **Page 65** Erica Echenberg/Redferns. **Page 66** LFI. **Page 67** Steve Morley/Redferns. **Page 68** LFI. **Pages 68-69** Steve Morley/Redferns. **Pages 70-1** Redferns. **Page 72** Keith Bernstein/Redferns. **Pages 74-5** Ian Dickson/Redferns. **Pages 76-7** LFI. **Page 77** Courtesy of Polydor Records. **Pages 78-9** Erica Echenberg/Redferns. **Page 80** (t) Courtesy of Polydor Records; (b) Keith Bernstein/Redferns. **Pages 80-1** Keith Bernstein/Redferns. **Pages 82-3** Ebet Roberts/Redferns. **Page 83** Courtesy of Polydor Records. **Page 85** (t) Ebet Roberts/Redferns; (b) Simon Fowler/LFI. **Page 86** Peter Mazel/LFI. **Page 88**. **Page 89** Erica Echenberg/Redferns. **Page 93** Redferns.

Every effort has been made to contact copyright holders. If any ommissions do occur the Publisher would be delighted to give full credit in subsequent reprints and editions.